DECODABLE BOOK 1

Orlando   Boston   Dallas   Chicago   San Diego

Visit *The Learning Site!*

www.harcourtschool.com

D0066880

Printed in the United States of America

ISBN 0-15-326681-3

15 179 10 09 08 07

Ordering Options
ISBN 0-15-323767-8 (Collection)
ISBN 0-15-326715-1 (package of 5)

Contents

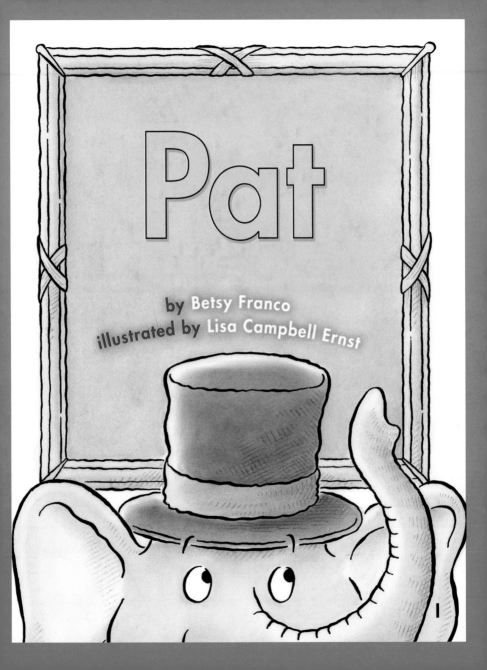

Pat

by Betsy Franco
illustrated by Lisa Campbell Ernst

1

I am Pat.

Pat sat. Go, Pat!

Pat sat. Go, Pat!

Pat sat. Go, Cat!

What can Pat do?

Pat can tap!

Tap, tap, tap!

8

Nan Cat!

by J.C. Cunningham
illustrated by Michael Grejniec

Come here, Nan!

Nan Cat sat.

Come here, Nan!

12

Nan Cat sat up.

I am sad, Nan.

Nan! Nan!

Look at Nan Cat!

Pat

Word Count: 26

High-Frequency Words

do
go
what

Decodable Words*

am
can
Cat
I
Pat
sat
tap

*Words with /a/*a* appear in **boldface** type.

Nan Cat!

Word Count: 25

High-Frequency Words

come
here
look
up

Decodable Words*

am
at
Cat
I
Nan
sad
sat

*Words with /a/*a* appear in **boldface** type.